I0617359

IF I LISTEN, I CAN HEAR

THE INSPIRATION WITHIN

JAMES R. MUNDAY

Quantum
Discovery
A LITERARY AGENCY

ISBN
978-1-959314-67-7 (Paperback)
978-1-959314-68-4 (eBook)

JAMES R. MUNDAY

IF I LISTEN, I CAN HEAR

THE INSPIRATION WITHIN

TABLE OF CONTENTS

When I read the title of Ron's book: *If I Listen, I Can Hear,* I immediately knew he had a message. I spent 45 of the happiest years of my life as a teacher, counselor and school principal. I learned early at every stage of my career the value of listening. To listen is not enough, you have to truly hear to get the message and I think Ron has done this. The sensitivity of each poem shows and you know that he has a deep yearning to hear the message that his Heavenly Father is sending.

After reading all his poems, I think he has achieved his goal and not only listened, he heard and has been able to pass that love and understanding on to his readers.

Doris Gerron
Retired School Administrator
Ennis, TX

I have known Ron since we were teenagers and have always known him to be forthright, honest and of highest integrity. I have observed first-hand over many years that through the culmination of his loving family, multiple professional endeavors and his undying faith in God, he has achieved these profound poems. They are truly sincere works embroiled in life's everyday struggles, inspired by the Spirit and consummated in his belief in Eternal Life.

Tom Wilkes
Ovilla, TX

Having had the opportunity to read over these impressive, meaningful and spectacular poems, it is very evident that endless hours of love and thought went into these writings.

Carma Thomas
Computer Lab Aide
Ennis, TX

FOREWORD

I first met Ron Munday when he was the Health Officer for the city of Ennis and I was principal of W.B. Travis Elementary School there. I had occasion to call on him for assistance and he worked tirelessly to solve the problem. I knew then that he was a person who gave all he had to solve problems and help others in any way he could.

I am sure Ron would be the first to tell you that the person he is today is a combination of the students and teachers he worked with when he was teaching and coaching, the many co-workers he was associated with and the multitude of owners of businesses he served as Health Officer, his loving wife, Janet, and his daughters as well as his extended family and friends. All of these people and experiences have contributed to the man he is today.

Finally, Ron would give credit to his Heavenly Father for being there during his journey to becoming a man. He was with him during his serious illness and Ron called on Him to see him through the dark days and nights. He heard his prayers and the close relationship made him the vessel for his book of poetry.

Doris Gerron
Retired School Administrator
Ennis, TX

I first met Ron Munday when he came to help me coach the men's basketball team at Southwestern Assemblies of God University. Ron won the confidence of my players and me with his consuming desire to help wherever he could. He was a constant source of encouragement to everyone that came into contact with him. His long years of experience in the coaching field were an asset to us during that season. I did not know the poet side of him until the end of the season when he brought me a framed poem that he had completed and gave it to me as a gift. I still have it in my office and when I read it occasionally, it gives me com comfort while dealing with the high pressure that comes with college athletics. I see in his writings a sensitivity to the hand of God that I believe is truly working in his life. It has been my pleasure to be a colleague and friend and I recommend this collection of verse to you.

Dr. Jerry Boone
Athletic Director-Head Men's Basketball Coach
Southwestern Assemblies of God University
Waxahachie, Texas

INTRODUCTION

As I awoke early one morning in January 2001, I had barely slept for days or even weeks. I sat in my chair feeling very ill from a chronic digestive disorder that seemed to have revenge on my body. Having lost thirty-five pounds in the last four months, I felt very ill and nauseated. I would have given anything to just sleep for a few hours. As I sat there I felt at the same time, both illness and a sense of peace. Odd, I thought, but nevertheless, I felt something in my soul. I didn't really want to lose any weight. I had only weighed 195 pounds when all this started. I found it difficult to eat and I felt something was very wrong within my body. Having been through about every test available, my doctor could not tell me much. The nights were really restless and I was afraid to go to sleep. Once asleep, I would abruptly be awaken by a deficiency of oxygen.

This was horrifying to me and my thought process. It brought me to the brink of dying. Or so I thought. During these moments of trying to catch my breath, I would struggle to the point of total exhaustion. Finally with much relief, I would slowly catch a small breath of air. In this frantic moment which seemed to last for a long period, my wife beside me and just as afraid as myself, I began to breath again. After a cold washcloth and some encouragement from my wife, I would try to sleep. Of course I was totally exhausted by now and afraid to sleep. This went on for months and it seemed there was nothing that could be done to alleviate this disorder. During this time I found my peace in God. I'm not sure how I found this peace, but I felt whatever was about happen, I could deal with it. Maybe it was God's will that I suffer this ordeal. I just knew asphyxiation was not the way anyone wants to go.

During this illness I spent much of my time in prayer. Not just prayer, but perpetual prayer. As I encountered going to bed each night, I had a keen sense of not wanting to go to sleep. I call it fear. So I began to pray and time seemed to stop. Each night seemed to last forever. I tried to put myself in the presence of the Lord. During my prayer I would just stop and try to feel the Lord. This would last until the alarm would go off. Again, total exhaustion. However, this kept me breathing and alive. I began to trust the Lord that I would conquer this disease. It continued and I kept up the process of prayer. On this particular morning in January, I laid there in deep prayer and the word cascade kept coming to mind. Cascade. That was what I was going through, a cascade of life, a cascade of the gift of life by God. This cascade also wasabout the strife in my life and the innocence and loss of my childhood. This cascade was about me and my life. I was ready for anything now. This cascade was about the blessings of my life, however difficult this would be it was my cascade. As I sat in my chair that morning I felt that I had something to do. This was about me and my relationship with God. I grabbed a pen and a notebook and a cascade of words echoed my thoughts. I wrote the poem Cascade on this January morning. It just seemed to jump on the paper. It was as if something or someone had helped me write this. As I read Cascade over and over I felt peace. Peace during crisis. It felt good. I read Cascade over several times that day and I felt the presence of God in my writing. I knew this Cascade would continue in my life and whatever God had in store for me, I was ready. I had no visions of writing again, or at least had no plans to, but God would continue to bless me with more. As the days went on I continued to struggle with my physical problems and of course I still went through my daily and nightly perpetual prayer process. God had something more for me and my life was ready for it. This writing gave me hope for my life. I had always felt that God had anointed people to do certain things in their lives, but I had never imagined that God wanted me to write poems to share with the masses. Maybe this was what God had planned for me from the very beginning. However, I never knew what I was to write or if I would be inspired to write again. It was something I didn't think much about. I just seemed to come up with ideas during the day doing mundane things and the titles came to me as if a wind had blown them to me. As I began to write more poems I knew something special was happening to me. It was a blessing from God and the Holy Sprit had touched me in a way that would change me and my life. I had indeed found peace and trust in the Lord. I continued to write the poems in this book and feel blessed and humbled to share these with you. These spiritual poems have a voice and the voice speaks from the person that reads it. The song "All You Need is Love" was right on. All we need is love from our God and the love of our friends and family. In Romans 13:10, God commands us that love is the answer to every one of the commandments. May the peace of God be with you also. As the days and months went by I continued to write more poems. I stayed in a state of perpetual prayer during my time that I was supposed to be sleeping. I continued to have the episodes where the acid from my stomach would come up into my throat and thus the near asphyxiation would occur. I fought it off with prayer and supposition to the Lord I knew. I was just thankful for the blessings I have and for my family, the most important thing to me. I wrote "If I Listen" late one night and felt that God was near to my heart. All the time that I had spent in prayer had led me to believe that "If I Listen, I Can Hear" (The Inspiration Within).

A REASON TO BELIEVE

A reason to believe, a season of doubt.
Endless thoughts, thrown about.
A race to run until the end,
Infinite beginning to an endless end.
A sun that sets, a wind that blows,
A reason to believe, blessings behold.
The leaves that fall, a gift from God.
All things from heaven waiting to unfold.

A reason to believe, from day to day,
Joy at least, the children play.
In the eyes of a child I see,
The love of a mother, her grace and ease.
Just a reason to believe, Thy love and faith,
I'm drawn to my knees.
Another reason to believe.

A reason to believe, a life to live,
Upon the cross, death for our sins.
Saved by faith, the Prince of Peace,
A reason to believe, until life's end.
So each day passes, redemption so near,
Love for your family, the ones most dear.
So run the race until the end,
God's eternal light will shine within.

ALONG THE WAY

I found myself along the way,
Eternity in balance, amidst the shadow of my days.
Left wondering an endless wave,
Life's path has veered and swayed.
Aimless at times, mindless and blind,
Lost in confusion, the emptiness of time.
Along the way I stopped to pray,
A road I crossed, far and away.
Still in tack, my faith in hand,
My journey unfinished, here and again.
My wonderment of man, with heaven in command.

I heard Him say, you're just a man.
Humble and meek, my humility complete.
Once again, I'm near defeat.
Along the way, I heard Him say,

Trust in Me, the righteous way.
Though I'm lost, at least it seems,
Maybe there's hope in my dreams.
Down a long road, a path I've crossed,
A wrong turn indeed, I must confess.
Along the way, He made the way,
For people like me to find His way.
Upon the mountain, I must have fell,
Into a valley, a dark despair.
Only to find that in the end,
He was beside me, holding my hand.

CASCADE

A cascade of showers upon my head
From where it came a distant despair.
Dark as night, or light as day
This love of life yearns to stay.

If by chance or fate of one
Awesome as a setting sun.
This cascade of warmth is now and again
Much as the soul that abides within.

I gaze into this genesis of mine,
As if to say it's not my time.
Forever is now, and so it will be;
There is something greater for all to see.

If in the clouds or up and beyond,
This dimension envisioned is surely the one.
With this cascade so well in hand,
As if the wind blows by His command.

A water fall of beauty and master of the plan,
Felt by the touch of His majestic hand.

Distinction of pain unwelcome by its fame,
Without a thought, I say His name.

It is simple, pure, and plain
As a gentle rain.
A cascade of dark, a shimmer of light,
One must choose his own life's part.

If by the wind, it is His breath,
Or raindrops that fall it comes to rest.
Upon this land I weep or reap,
As if in a thundercloud or the ocean deep.

Life is short or just so long,
As He will enlighten me with His song.
Not to be timid as if a lost soul,
The cascade of life is one for the bold.

With His hand He comforts me,
By the art of His simplicity.
Upon this throne, I'm sure He sits,
With hope and love I'll need His rest.

A cascade of rain that once fell,
Will in the end, be a crown upon my head.

IF I LISTEN

If I listen, I can hear,
Words so soft, a gentle tear.
Word for word, thought for thought,
I listen intently, near and far.

Quiet as the morning dew,
Soft and warm, from Me to you.
If I listen, I can hear.
The words You speak, have no fear.

If I listen, I can hear,
Your love I hold so dear.
Little by little You let me know,
Seasons pass, as I grow old.
Love, Faith, Hope, and Grace,
You taught me these from an early age.

But there's so much more I want to know,
My wish is that You will show me more.

To be kind, to show love,
To be thoughtful of the ones I love.
If I listen, I can hear,
Words of wisdom from You, my Lord,
These I hold most dear.

LIFE IS FOREVER

Life is forever this I'm told,
A story unending, yet to unfold.
From life's beginning, until one's end
Eternal bliss waiting, forever and then.

From mountaintops above, the valleys within,
heartfelt emotion once and again.
Life is forever, as the essence of time,
Words of wisdom etched upon my mind.
On the wings of an angel His voice will come,
To silence us all upon His Return.
Blessings abound, His Presence profound,
Up into Heaven with a thunderous sound.

Life is forever, Eternity near,
He is patiently waiting, just have no fear.
For Life is forever and oh so dear,

So Life is forever, this I'm told,
This blissful peace will enter my soul.

MASTERPIECE
FROM HEAVEN

Masterpiece from Heaven, a gift from above.
Born unto salvation, the Son of God.
A stream that flows steady and pure.
Jesus the man, the rock of Love.
Given unto man, the Light that shines.
Not that we deserve, this act so kind.
Masterpiece from Heaven, a song He sings.
Miracles abound, and unending dream.
Clouds that move across an endless sky.
A sun that sets, an unending fire.
Words that speak of truth and love.
Wisdom and faith, the warmth of His embrace.

Masterpiece from Heaven, a lesson of love.
Jesus spoke of these things I've heard.
Only by faith, I trust in Thee.
Winding down a path unseen.
Silent and dear, His voice so near.
Not to be heard, just felt I'm sure.
This Masterpiece of Heaven,
Gave His love to you and me.

OCEAN SO DEEP

Ocean so deep, with Heaven so high.
All humanity waiting, the glimpse of His eyes.
Out of the darkness, into the light.
Heaven and earth, a grand surprise.
On angels' wings, a restful sigh.
Teardrops falling from every man's eyes.

Ocean so deep, with Heaven so high.
Man's grasp for hope of the One Most High.
As a grain of sand on the shore.
Pulled from the bottom of the ocean's floor.
Caressed by the touch of His loving hands.
We're all just part of this masterful plan.

Ocean so deep, with Heaven so high.
Long sufferings end, a wonderful sight.
Out of the dark, an eternal light.
Son of man, Heaven's delight.
So up on a cloud, we're carried away.
Ocean so deep, a Heavenly stay.

ON THE JOURNEY TO FIND OUT

On the journey to find out,
Just what this life is about,
Down a slope, around a path,
Oh the roads I've traveled past.

Up and down the mountainside,
Down the valley, the still of enchantment inside.
All the twist and turns indeed,
The roads we cross, bring me to my knees.

Souls I've met, faces I've seen,
All in a pattern, a grand scheme.
On the journey to find out,
Seasons end and come about.

A gift from God, a risen dove,
Only to know His abundant Love.
The road is long and narrow I'm told,
Winding down a sojourn so bold.

Not by chance or fate it seems,
Life is a road of love and dreams.
Life is short, a story told,
Miracles abound within man's soul.

On the journey to find out,
Jesus the man crossed this path.

PLACE OF PEACE

Place of peace, so hard to find.
Clouds in the sky, moved by time.
If for a moment, His mysterious ways.
Lost in the clouds, far and away.

Beautiful medley amidst my eyes.
His name etched in the cloudburst of rhyme.
Distinction of the clouds, a heavenly style.
Only to be blown by the wind,
Each cloud lost to its form again.

Place of peace so hard to find.
Elusive thoughts for all mankind.
Serenity forever at least it seems,
Or just for a moment,
The sweetness of dreams.

His love abides in my soul,
Eternal promise written in prose.
Pristine as a waterfall in flow,
spectrum of light on my soul.
The sun that shines from above,
A place of peace, God above.
Place of peace, blown by the wind,
Wondering of my soul within.

Place of peace so hard to find,
The Lord will sanctify my mind.
Place of peace with faith and hope.
The harvest of the Lord,
Will enlighten my soul.

TIME IS WHISPERING IN THE WIND

Time is whispering in the wind,
eloquent silence, a heavenly realm.
Like a branch that holds its leaves,
for us all to blissfully see.

Strong and firm He holds my hand,
His touch as warm as a breeze of wind.
This mountain of love, no regret.
Faithful to the end, a distant sunset.

Gone in time with just a glance,
His love of life is not by chance.
Time is whispering in the wind,
as a spirit that dwells deep within.

Life after life, a promise made.
Silence of His voice, it is by grace.
The wind that blows is often cold,
His precious love is still untold.

This shadow of faith that I hold,
blown by nature tranquil yet bold.
Angels from heaven, a promise made,
that quiet whisper of faith is Heavenly made.

WHISPER IN THE WIND

Whisper in the wind,
Echoes that bring silence from within,
A voice so soft, nature can hear.
Only with hope and faith I hear within.

Whisper in the wind,
With angels from heaven and time at end,
Raindrops that fall, like a tear within,
Heaven is waiting, near the end.

A breath that blows,
A whisper in the wind,
A chasm that grows faith, deep within.
The Holy Spirit drifts again.

Love is brought with winds aloft,
A gentle touch, I know not when.
The essence of life, fought with strife,
Only to be saved by His presence and sight.
Oh how glorious this will be,
For all sinners to finally see.
The eyes of eternity forever to be.
Not just a whisper, a roar it seems,
Loud with thunder shimmering within
And always peaceful,
His gentle bliss again.

Oh I can hardly wait to see,
This whisper of wind,
A peaceful spirit dwells within.
Our Lord forever and ever again.

Whisper in the wind,
Angels and rainbows at last I'm a child again.
Our Lord has come once again,
A whisper of His Love drifts in the wind.

WITH SILENCE GOLDEN

Morning comes You enlighten me,
Without a word You comfort me.
Your silence golden, with thoughts of calm,
I know that soon You may come.

Your touch is subtle and oh so sweet,
On my knees I must retreat.
Back to Zion with wings abreast,
Tranquil solace upon to rest.

On this day I hope and pray,
Carry my soul up and far away,
With silence golden, I hope at best,
Carry us home for perpetual rest.

Love of life, life is love,
Heaven and treasure up above,
Through Your words of hope and faith,
I ask You now for Your grace.

With silence golden such as sleep,
Surely one day we will all meet.
Sunburst of love, hope and peace,
Woven unto man the Prince of Peace.

As we touch upon a cloud,
My heart will relish this reward.
With silence golden from above,
At last we see Your Abundant Love.

SPIRIT OF THE WIND

The wind that moves the Spirit aloft,
The clouds that bring peace to us,
Not to be seen but only felt.
The feeling of warmth, heavenly sent,
Love of the Spirit that abides within,
Wind that blows will come again.

A gentle strength, a gift from God,
The Holy Spirit that lives inside,
Quiet as the morning dew,
Caressed by a breeze from Him to you.
Divine as the light that shines on me,
The Spirit of the wind, yes I believe,
This gift from Heaven I accept,
Humble and meek the God I've met.

Spirit of the Wind, my life's in your hands,
Thankful Lord as I rest in Thee.
You come as often as I need.
As the wind that often blows,
My strength and character will only grow.
The Spirit of the Wind I believe,
Was sent from Heaven by God for me.

YOU ARE MY STRENGTH

You are my strength.

When I have grief, You take half of it.
It is halved between us.

When I have hope, I give you half of it.
Then we have hope together.

You are my strength.

When I have lost, You help me find.
When I have won, you share my prize.

You give me strength when I am weak.
It's so easy, God sent you to me.

He is my strength.

I CAN ONLY IMAGINE

I can only imagine the gifts of God,
Heaven, Serenity, Peace and Love.
All that is and all that will be,
If only now man could see.
His peace and love forever will be,
I know not what to think.
The nature of God's love and peace,
Given to me as free as the wind.
I can only wait for salvation to begin.

I can only imagine what Jesus said,
To all the masses on earth back then.
Though He walked as a common man,
He spoke of heavenly things man did not understand.
How I wish I were there to witness,
His miracles and touch His hand.
How He must have felt sharing His love and hope,

Only to be put on the cross for all to see,
Humble in His death for you and me.

I can only imagine how God must have felt,
To see His Son on the cross put to death.
Loss of life, complete in strife, oh but risen and then,
Jubilation in Heaven and on Earth again.
Jesus has Risen, surely we should praise Him,
Not just now, but forever and in the end,
He will be there, the trust we heed.
Forever in Heaven to meet our needs,
God is there just pray on your knees.

I can only imagine how Heaven will be,
so much love and our God to see.
Up into heaven and eternal bliss,
My hope is we deserve this amazing gift.
Though I wait and endure the pain,
Of all these earthly things.
I put my faith and trust in God,
In His perpetual love for you and me,
I can only imagine how Heaven will be.

MOUNTAIN OF LOVE

Mountain of Love, Valley of Hope,
All corridors therein, lead to God's Love.
From far away to near one's heart,
To hear His calling, to listen from the heart.
Up so high on mountain's top,
Down so low in valley's depth.
So many paths, oh so many roads,
Ones I've crossed, twisted at redemption road,
Only to be touched by God's special Love.

Mountain of Love, Valley of Hope,
I crossed a path, straight and true.
By grace of God I walked the valleys dew,
I traverse up the mountain near to You.
The walk of Life seems so long,
The blink of an eye to our God's sense of time.

Each one walks his special way,
Some in a dark, dismal gray.

Mountain of Love, Valley of Hope,
Caressed by the light of God that shines on all.
Magenta sky, the end of a day,
All my wonder and hope I see in Jesus Christ.
Waterfall of Glory, spectrum of eternal light,
One must choose his purpose in life,
One must accept Glory and Strife.
Mountain of Love, Valley of Hope,
Heaven's door open to the soul.
Roads I've crossed, have two paths,
One I choose leads astray,
One I choose is Heaven's Way.
God the Mountain of Love,
Jesus Christ the Valley of Hope.
With Love and Hope in my heart,
I know Jesus Christ will never part.

THE TOUCH OF GOD

The Touch of God upon my hands, my soul,
my heart, He surrounds.
Heaven and Earth all abound,
Upon my soul God has found.

Stars across a night so still, a wind that blows.
The leaves that fall, each unique in
their shape and size.
Not to be cast adrift, as the leaves in flight,
But sent with direction, much like a sunrise.
Always there, but not to be touched.
Such as a cloud, it's endless shroud.

The Touch of God upon my soul.
He who has made me whole.
Just this life and so much more.

But I seem so small when I compare,
All the things that God has made.
Perfect in His special way,
Oh the Love that is so great.
He is what has come over me.
I see His perfection in all that's made.
Not an illusion, this I'm sure,
The Touch of God, His grand parade.

The Touch of God, His special place,
His Heaven, His Earth, His Space.
A river that flows, a tree that grows,
The smile of a child, a parent so proud.
Ocean's wave, men so brave,
All a part of what is good, God has made.

The Touch of God, a beautiful flower,
Into spring it grows. All the children
I watch them grow, so much love, this I know.
The Touch of God is over me,
I see it in my childrens' dreams.

The birds that fly against an endless sky,
A snow that falls across a mountain side.
The warmth of a breeze across my face,
A cool running stream, into a beautiful lake.
I seem to know where it came,
Hope all mankind is sure of the same.

The Touch of God, His Son on a cross,
Came for salvation to touch all of us.
Blessed are we in our lives,
To be touched by God, our Hope and Relief.
So, on a cloud His Presence known,
He will come to invite us into His home.
Up into heaven and near His Throne.

Loud with thunder, His approach,
Out of Heaven to take my soul.
The Touch of God, if I can wait,
Will one day be a gift for all to take.
The Touch of God, His final gift,
Music from heaven for all mankind.

Our God is real.
Man cannot hide what God has made.
He gave us eyes so we can see,
The Touch of God is real indeed.

THE EYES OF GOD

The Eyes of God that gaze upon my soul,
my words, my thoughts, the tears untold.
He hears my voice before I speak,
knows the rhythm of my heartbeats.
Sees the sun before it will rise,
lets the clouds drift, an endless sky.
He will return with great surprise,
for all mankind, our spirit will rise,
heaven's gate, a look into God's eyes.

The Eyes of God that gaze upon my soul,
all of Heaven and Earth will surely know.
For the Eyes of God have seen me fall,
upon my face, I've seen it all.
Love, Hate, and all it seems,
surely God's grace will redeem us all.

He sees the good that I have done,
just a miracle of the Enlightened One.
A realm of light for all to see,
I only know He watches over me.
All my days, and all my nights,
a gentle rain, a tearful thought.

The Eyes of God that gaze upon my soul,
my love, my hope, waiting to unfold.
All my dreams, my despair, as rain from Heaven,
we all know a God that shares.
For His love, His strength, my trust,
in Him is most complete.
Upon my mountain of grace and hope,
the Eyes of God will search my soul.
From His place in Heaven above,
the Eyes of God will cleanse my soul.

CLOUDS FROM HEAVEN

Clouds from Heaven perched by the wind,
soft and quiet, a whisper on a whim.
As beautiful as a morning sunrise,
Lighted by moonlight at night.
Enchanted by the clouds of life.
Across the midst of a dark blue sky,
I've fallen into God's restful sigh,
to see the beauty and the awe.
This handiwork from Heaven,
Tears in my eyes.

Clouds from Heaven lifted by His hand,
caressed by God on a restless wind.
As He lifts the clouds so high,
my heart soars to their shape and size.
So this breeze that blows them away.

My Lord will receive my humble praise.
Though He speaks through His works,
He has made our Heaven and Earth.
Clouds from Heaven, a gift from God,
Lifted into Heaven, by the Hand of God.

HE THAT HELD MY HAND

He that held my hand,
Through life's rain and storm.
Down a river of thought and tribulation,
Only to be brought to a shimmer of light.
Not an ending, but a grand beginning.

He that held my hand,
Through the darkness of dreams.
Into a light shining as one,
Each step taken by all who walk.
As tears from heaven slowly drop.

He that holds my hand,
As a soul deep in thought.
Restless as a wind that blows,
His constant grip upon my soul.
He that held my hand,
Was God and His master plan.